THE ANSWER

COPING WITH CRITICISM

A PRACTICAL GUIDE FOR TRANSFORMING

CRITICISM INTO PERSONAL GROWTH

Neal Carboneau

The Answer - Coping With Criticism:
A Practical Guide For Transforming
Criticism Into Personal Growth
Copyright © 2024 by Neal Carboneau

Published by Neal Carboneau

ISBN 979-8-218-52788-4

Neal Carboneau can be contacted at P.O. Box 251, Three Oaks, Michigan 49128, or by email at Neal@NealCarboneau.com

Comments from Early Reviewers

"WOW!"
"Love it!"
"I think your book is incredible!"
"It's very good."

Table of Contents

Introduction

This book is intended to provide simple solutions to a complex problem.

Hopefully, it will be funny, memorable and easy to do.

Take your time, do a little at a time, come back and review, then continue. Be sure to take notes and work through the exercises as you go. It will make it much easier to relate and remember.

Other helpful information is held off until the end of the book, so you can get right to

The Answer

How do you cope with criticism?

1st Catch yourself reacting to a comment.

2nd Reframe it.

3rd Get some Air, take a breath, find a way to get away.

4th Do a Post event review.

Yep, it's CRAP.

The next time you start to react to a negative comment or situation, say

"oh CRAP, here we go again." (Preferably to yourself)

Remember

Catch yourself

Reframe it

Air, get some air,

 take a breath, get away

Post event review

Catch Yourself

What are some things you do, feel or think when someone has made a critical comment to you?

Write them down here or another convenient spot.

Start a Journal

_____

_____

_____

_____

Are your examples here?

- Your face or neck gets flush.
  - You feel warmth or redness in your face.
  - You feel anger or embarrassment.
- Your mind starts churning.
  - You have racing thoughts.
  - You're thinking about how to respond.
- Your jaw may clench.
  - You feel that tension or stress.
- You start to sweat.
- Your chest feels tight.
- You might even start shaking or trembling.

Wow. I'm starting to feel this way just thinking about it.

Are you?

That's how to know how to catch yourself.

The Fight or Flight Response

It's instinct. The criticism is seen as a threat. Your body reacts the same way as if it's in real danger by triggering a flood of stress hormones and other reactions.

Fight   Flight

Here's a few examples

- You might start fidgeting:
  - Playing with your hair,
  - Wringing your hands.
- Your stomach feels tense.
- You may have difficulty concentrating:
  - Your mind is racing and replaying the comment.

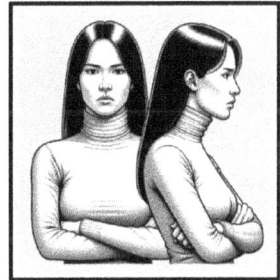

- You've lost your focus.
- You may start to raise your voice.
- You might cross your arms or hunch your shoulders.

Can you think of any more reactions you've had when criticized? Write them down.

Reframe it

Reframing is just another way of thinking.

Let's take the anxiety we felt thinking about our reactions.

Notice that nothing is happening, you just read something that made you feel anxious. So by looking at this for what it is, a harmless exercise that's stirring up negative thoughts from a previous situation, you are taking the second step in coping with criticism.

Here are some ways to help when you've been criticized.

We'll start with ways to think about the other person, in the moment, to lessen the impact.

Ask yourself why the person acted the way they did.

Here are some examples:

- Misplaced anger

  They might be angry or frustrated about something other than you. But, they're taking it out on you because you're a convenient target.

- Personal issues or stress

  They could be going through a tough time. Their actions are a reflection of their struggles not you.

- Feeling threatened

  They might feel threatened for some reason. It could be their fight or flight reaction causing them to criticize and assert their dominance.

- Lack of self awareness or empathy

  Some people may not understand how their words or actions affect others. They may be unintentionally hurtful or insensitive.

Here are a few more:

- Jealousy or envy

  The person may feel threatened by your appearance, success, abilities, or possessions, leading them to lash out in an attempt to diminish your achievements.

- Competitiveness

  In some cases, criticism may be a way for the person to gain a competitive edge or make themselves feel superior.

- Power and dominance

  The person may use criticism or meanness as a way to assert their power, control others, or gain a higher social standing. This behavior often stems from underlying insecurities or a need for dominance.

- Attention seeking

  Some people may use criticism or mean spirited comments as a way to get attention or provoke a reaction from others.

They may have acted that way out of

- Perfectionism

  If the person holds themselves or others to unrealistically high standards, they may be overly critical of any perceived flaws or mistakes.

- Learned behavior

  The individual may have grown up in an environment where criticism and negativity were normal. They may be repeating things they experienced in childhood.

- Projection

  The individual may be projecting their own insecurities, fears, or weaknesses onto you, criticizing you for things they dislike about themselves.

Let's think about these a little more

You were probably thinking about situations you have had that fit these descriptions.

Take a few minutes to go back to the top of this list starting with "Misplaced Anger." Read through each one again and write down a situation and person that applies to each example.

You can use the space on each page, the note page or a journal.   It will help you learn reframing. The more you practice, the better you'll get.

Understanding Emotional Detachment

When we're faced with tough situations, especially when someone's criticizing us, our brain might try to protect us by emotionally detaching. This is also called dissociation. It's like your mind hits the pause button on your feelings to help you get through a stressful moment.

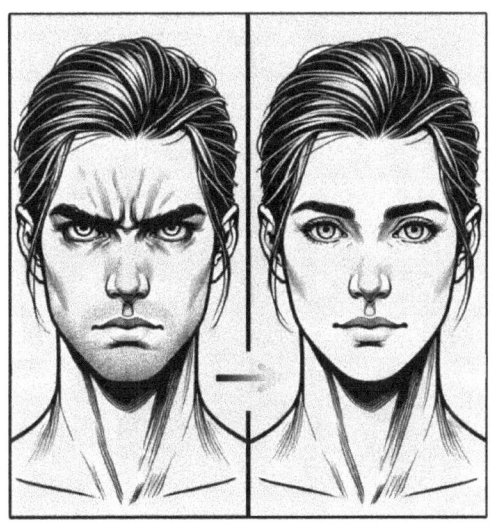

This might sound like a good thing at first. After all, who wouldn't want to avoid feeling hurt or upset? But here's the catch, while it might help in the short term, it can cause problems down the road.

The Upside of Detaching

Emotional detachment can be a quick fix when you're feeling overwhelmed. It can:

- Give you a break from intense feelings
- Help you stay calm in heated situations
- Stop you from saying something you might regret later

But remember, it's like putting a band aid on a deep cut. It might stop the bleeding a little, but it won't heal the wound.

The Downside of Checking Out Emotionally

While it might feel good to 'check out' emotionally in the moment, there are some downsides:

Missing Out on Understanding:

When you detach, you might miss important cues about what the other person is really trying to say. It's like trying to read a book with your eyes closed.

Communication Breakdown:

If you're not fully 'there' emotionally, it's hard to express yourself clearly. This can lead to misunderstandings and make the situation worse.

Increases the Replay:

Have you replayed a situation in your mind later?
Thinking about what you could have said?

- It becomes a negative spiral.
- Detaching can make this worse.
- If we don't process the emotions in the moment, our brain keeps trying to figure it out later.

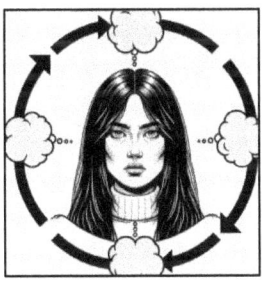

Problem Solving is Harder:

Emotions play a big role in how we solve problems, especially with other people. If you're emotionally checked out, you might miss out on finding a good solution.

A Better Way Forward

So, what can you do instead of detaching?

Here are some ideas:

Stay Present:

Use the breathing techniques we talked about earlier to help you stay grounded in the moment.

Name those Feelings:

Try to identify what you're feeling:

- Anger
- Hurt
- Anxiety
- Fear

Just naming the emotion can help you manage it better. Practice Empathy:

Empathy just means authentically caring for the other person. Trying to understand where the other person is coming from. This doesn't mean you have to agree with them, or even like them, but it can help you respond in a more constructive way.

Remember to say "oh CRAP, here we go again," and catch yourself, reframe it, get some air or get away, then do your post event review.

This can help you stay in the moment without getting overwhelmed.

If you find yourself detaching often, it might be helpful to talk to someone. Several resources are discussed later. They can give you more tools to handle the tough situations.

Remember, learning to stay emotionally present isn't easy, but it's worth it. It can lead to better communication, stronger relationships, positive outcomes and a deeper understanding of yourself and others. Keep practicing, you'll get there.

Air

Are you still feeling anxious?

The next step can be used in the moment or anytime you need to relax.

What does "Air" mean?

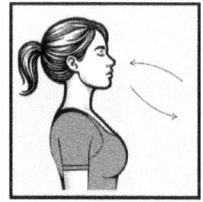

- Get some air, take a breath.

  In the moment, try to force yourself to take a few breaths and relax.

  (You don't need to be obvious about it)

- Get away if you can.

  Make an excuse if you need to. Buy yourself some time to regroup or get some help.

- Relax.

  You caught yourself, you reframed it and you are in control. It can be hard, but try to relax while getting some air; especially, if you can't get away.

Deep Breathing

How do you do it?

The Box Method (Box Breathing) or Four Fours Method

- Inhale through your nose for a count of 4, focusing on expanding your stomach first, then your chest.

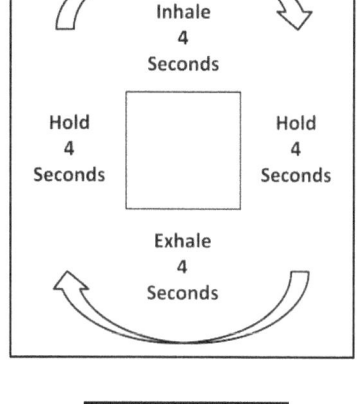

- Hold your breath for a count of 4. You will feel a hollow feeling in your solar plexus.

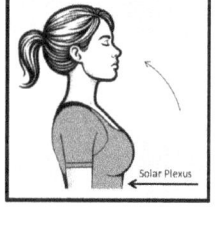

- Exhale slowly through your mouth for a count of 4.

- Hold for a count of 4 before inhaling again. You will feel that hollow feeling again.

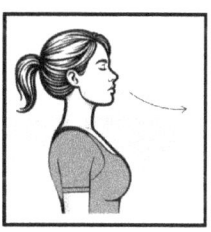

- Start to relax your body as you breathe. The relaxation guide is on the next page.

Close your eyes if you can and repeat several times until you feel your body and mind start to relax.

Relax

- Starting with your face try to feel yourself relax your brow, jaw and face.

    The key is feeling the relaxation.

- Feel your neck, shoulders and back relax.

- Keep box breathing.

- Feel your arms and hands relax.

- Try to feel your heart relax.

    Feel that hollowness in your solar plexus.

- Try relaxing your lungs and stomach.

- Relax your belly.

- Relax your back muscles.

- Relax your legs and feet.

Practice Makes Perfect

Go through the steps several times, and remember to use them any time you need to.

Did it help?

- First think about how you are feeling right now.

- What's your facial expression?

- Are any of your muscles tense?

- Can you feel your clothing, what you are sitting on?

- Are you still a little anxious from your thoughts about previous encounters?

- Read back through the breathing and relaxation steps and do them several more times.

Did some of your anxiety go away after doing the breathing and relaxation exercises a few times?

Think about how much these techniques will help you in the future:

- In the moment,

- Later when you are thinking back on the situation,

- When you just need to relax.

Maybe even when trying to go to sleep at night.

There are a number of benefits.

Focus is another benefit.

Do you feel more focused?

A Side Note - Focus and Memory

Jim Kwik has a book titled, "Limitless." In it he talks about ways to improve your memory and learn more.

The breathing exercises and relaxation techniques help you get in the "zone" or "flow state."

It's why you may feel more alert now.

Some other simple strategies he mentions to help you learn and remember include breaking the time you spend into smaller parts, say 20 minutes at a time with a quick break. But, don't refocus on something else because that will defeat the purpose.

He also talks about repetition.

Don't just use this book once.

Go back through it often.

Think about those situations you have been in before.

It will help you learn the reasons better and be able to react faster in the future, when being criticized.

Self awareness is another excellent way to monitor and control your actions. We'll talk more about that later.

Post

The post event review:

This is an important step in coping and managing your response to the criticism. It's an opportunity to reflect on the situation, your reactions, your feelings, the hurt it caused, start healing and prepare for the next time.

Fight or flight was mentioned earlier. It takes over when we are criticized because our bodies feel and react to the threat as though we are in real danger.

Fight   Flight

The steps in catching ourselves, reframing and taking a breath are all in an effort to take back control from our instinct.

C

R

A

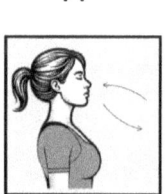

. P

A critical part of the post event review is getting control, understanding what happened and why.

You know how we discussed the replay earlier.

Sometimes it goes on and on.

That negative spiral just gets worse.

Our mind just keeps replaying the event, ruminating.

It's hard to just shut it off, but you can manage it.

You need to take back control.

It's a good time to say "oh, CRAP here I go again."

Catch yourself in the negative spiral.

Reframe it.

It's not happening now.

Get some **A**ir.

Do your breathing and
relaxation exercises.

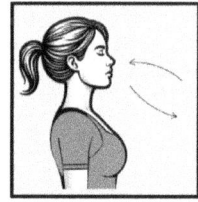

Then start your **P**ost event review.

Steps in the Post Event Review

These will help you start the healing process and take control of your reactions.

- Do it alone, relax and focus.

  Do the breathing and relaxation exercises to get yourself in the right frame of mind.

- Replay the event.

  Close your eyes and mentally replay the event as if you were watching a movie. Try to observe the situation without judgment, focusing on what happened.

- Identify your triggers.

  Think about the specific words, actions, expressions or circumstances that triggered your response.

  Was it the tone of voice, the words?

  Write it down.

Journaling is an excellent way to recover, remember and learn for the future.

- Think about your emotions.

  It's ok to have reacted the way you did.

  Forgive yourself.

  Remember, our instinct takes control and the more we understand, reflect and practice the better we'll get, in the moment.

- Write down how you felt:

    Hurt, angry, embarrassed, or defensive?

- Don't judge yourself, just realize how it made you feel.

- Evaluate your reaction:

  Consider how you reacted to the situation.

  Did you respond calmly and professionally?
  Did your emotions get the best of you?

- Were you able to say "oh CRAP, here we go again" and use techniques you learned?

  Did you Catch yourself?

  Were you able to Reframe it?

  Could you quickly relax and take a breath?

  Were you able to get away to regroup?

- Try reframing it again while doing the Post.

  Use the reframing section. Review the list of reasons the person may have acted the way they did. Write them down.

- Evaluate the situation:

  Did you do something that they misunderstood?

  Was it actually constructive criticism?

  Thinking back, did the person have good intentions and just a bad way of saying it?

  How can you grow from the situation?

In the reframing section, we talked about just blaming the other person. It allows you to better handle the situation in the moment, but to truly grow and get better, it's important to learn from each situation.

Did the person actually mean well, but did a poor job expressing it?

Do you think you misunderstood or misread the situation?

Do you think you overreacted?

Remember, be kind to yourself. You did the best you could in the moment.

I've been studying these techniques for more than twenty five years and I still struggle from time to time.

It's about continuous improvement, getting better each time.

Life Long Learning

Reacting Better in the Future

- Practice active listening.

  When receiving criticism, focus on understanding the other person's perspective and message.

  Ask questions and repeat what you heard to make sure you understand what they are saying.

  People often say, "they weren't even listening to me." Have you felt that way?

- Try to respond, not react.

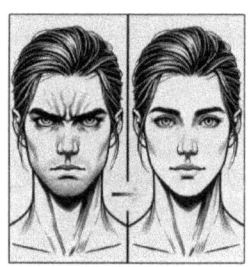

- Stay emotionally connected, unless it's an extreme situation.

- Set boundaries:

  If the criticism becomes abusive, excessive, or unproductive, it's important to set clear boundaries. Here's an example of what to say:

I understand you're frustrated, but it's not acceptable to speak to us that way. We deserve to be treated with respect, just as we try to treat you with respect. Let's start over and talk through this respectfully. If you need a few minutes to collect your thoughts, please take it, and I will be here to work through it with you.

Non Verbal Cues

What you don't say impacts the conversation.

Think about:

- The expression on your face,
- What your body language is saying,
- Your tone of voice.

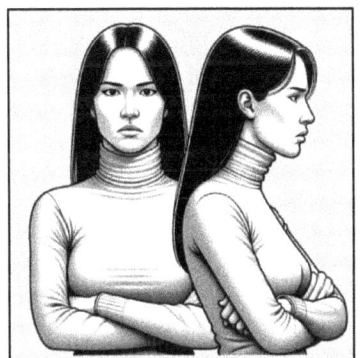

What's your facial expression right now?

Thinking about your non verbal cues is a good habit to get into.

Catch yourself doing other things.

Think about your expression, what gestures you are making? What tone of voice you are using?

The more often you catch yourself and think these through, the better you'll get.

Getting Help

After your post event review, if you thought about things that are not covered here, look for additional help.

You could search the internet for the specific question or topic you want more help with.

I talk later about how much of a help artificial intelligence (Ai) has been for me. Antrhopic's Claude, Open Ai's Chat GPT, Google's Gemini and Microsoft's Copilot have all been instrumental in helping me research and better explain strategies I have learned throughout my life.

Ask one of them your question. I think you will be amazed at their responses. I was.

You can talk to your supervisor or someone you see as a mentor, or just talk through it with a friend.

A number of psychological principles are discussed here. It's not intended to replace professional help. Know that there are a number of sources for specific help including online therapy resources, Cognitive Behavioral Therapy and professionals in the field. Don't hesitate to get specialized help if you need it.

But, be sure to do the post event review first so that you have all of the information to evaluate the situation.

Moving Forward

There's a lot of information here. Learning to handle criticism is an ongoing process. Go back through this book often. By continuing to work through the strategies and exercises in your post event reviews and "training" yourself on how to act in the moment, you will continually improve your outcomes and resilience.

Topics on self awareness, confidence, assertiveness and humor can all help you improve your coping skills.

There are resources for additional help at the end of this book as well as YouTube videos on most of the topics you're interested in.

Each of these will help you develop greater resilience and confidence in the face of criticism.

You are stronger than you might think.

Celebrate your successes, practice, stay positive and allow the wound to heal.

- Look for the wins each time:

  Were you able to catch yourself?

  Could you reframe and relax enough to get out of the fight or flight mode?

  Was the amount of time you spent replaying the situation less than in the past?

  The less time you spend in the negative spiral, the more successful and faster your healing will be.

- Practice:

  Go back through this book often.

  Take notes right on the pages, or keep a journal.

  Think back through other situations.

  Try to better understand them based on the points made here.

If you find yourself struggling to move past a particularly challenging situation, don't hesitate to seek additional support. Dealing with criticism is a skill that can be learned and improved with practice and guidance.

Heal the Wound

Another important thing to know is that emotional injuries are very similar to physical injuries. They need to heal just like a cut. The post event review will help you through that healing process.

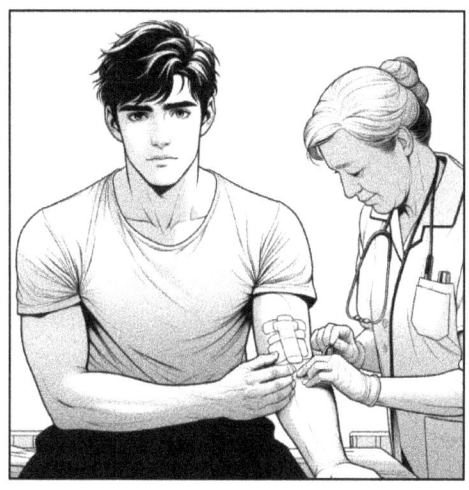

Remember, it takes time, just like healing a wound.

Give it a Try

It's a good time to work through some exercises to help remember.

Write down a few of the situations you've had in the past. Go back to the beginning of the book and think about each of these situations as you work through all of the steps until you get back here.

Write down your thoughts and answers in the book as you go. It will be a good reference in the future. Repetition is the key to remembering. The more times you go back through this book and work through the exercises, the better you'll get. It doesn't take long to get back to this point. Wear this book out. You will be glad you did.

Remember

Catch yourself if you start to get anxious about the thoughts.

Reframe the situation. You're not there. You are just thinking back through those situations.

Get some Air. Relax, breath and focus. Get in the right state of mind.

Post: Continue your efforts. Keep going back through to get better, learn more and become faster in the moment.

In the next section, we'll explore some common examples and take a deeper dive into additional strategies to help with coping and handling the situation as it happens.

Take a break. You've done a lot getting to this point. Come back later. Before you start again, go through the beginning of this book one more time to get better with the basics.

Example 1

(When you're ready)

These examples should help you respond in the future.

At Work

Your supervisor says, "what's taking so long?"

You instantly become defensive.

That's the fight or flight instinct.

You can't control it, but you can manage it.

Say, "Oh CRAP, here we go again."

Catch yourself reacting

Look back at the signs if you need a refresher:

- Flushing face, anger, racing heart.
- Not thinking clearly.
- It may be hard to answer well.

Know how we discussed thinking of things later you could have said?

It's because you are in the fight or flight mode.

But, you're getting better, you caught yourself.

Reframe it

Initially, just blame them in your mind
to get yourself in control.

Try to stay emotionally connected.

As you get better, you will be able to evaluate why they are acting that way, but for now, just blame them in your mind to get control of yourself.

- Their supervisor may have asked them when it was going to be done.
- They reacted poorly and came looking for you. They are in fight or flight mode.
- They could have said it in a better way.

Like, "hey the boss is wondering when we are going to be done. I know you've been double checking things to make sure they're right. How soon do you think you will be ready?"

You caught yourself and reframed it, now

Get some Air

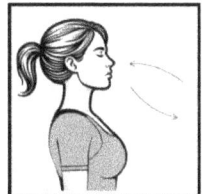

You may not be able to get away at that moment, so force yourself to relax. Feel the relaxation.

Take a few breaths, relax the best you can, and respond.

Try to soften your response so you don't make their fight or flight worse.

Try, "I'm just trying to finish something up here. Give me a few minutes. I'll come go through it with you."

This will give you a few more minutes to relax, get your thoughts, figure out what they need to know and how you can say it to help yourself, and help them.

Remember to do the Post

Relax, think back through the situation, how you felt, why you think they acted the way they did, what you said and what you could have said.

Write it down.

It will help you remember ways to respond in the future.

Example 2

A customer is very angry about quality

They are in an aggressive posture, squinted eyes, red face and say, "can't you do anything right?"

There goes your fight or flight.

Say, "Oh CRAP, here we go again."

Catch yourself

Reframe it

They are angry at the situation, not you.

or

They could just be a mean person.

Take a breath. Get some Air. Force yourself to relax. Feel it. Try to be as caring as you can.

De-Escalate

Buy yourself some time to relax, compose yourself, get some help and think about an appropriate response.

Say, "I'm sorry. I know how angry something like that can make me. Give me a second, let me get my supervisor and we'll figure this out for you."

- Soften the approach
- Listen
- Try to understand
- Repeat back the customer's concerns
- Use a calm tone of voice

Let your supervisor handle the situation if you can.

As you get better, you will feel more confident handling the situation yourself.

But, you can always buy yourself some time and get your supervisor.

When you get home, do a Post event review.

Ask yourself

How you felt?

Be honest with yourself.

- Scared?

- Were you concerned for your safety?

- Anxious, angry, defensive?

Don't judge.

You did the best you could at the time.

That's why you're here.

You're trying to get better.

All of these would be normal in a high stress situation.

Were you able to quickly reframe it and relax enough to get help?

Think about why the person might have been so angry

- Was the quality really bad?

- Could they have had a bad experience before?

- Are they just having a really bad day or dealing with personal issues?

Understanding their perspective can help you be more caring in the moment, even if they are acting inappropriately.

If your supervisor helped out, think about if they were able to:

- Express an understanding of the customer's feelings and the situation?

- Express a willingness to help?

- Set boundaries in the conversation?

- Support you while acknowledging the customer's feelings?

- Listen carefully to the customer's concerns?

- Repeat them back to show understanding?

- Use a calm tone of voice to de-escalate the situation?

These are all valuable skills that can be applied in the future.

Think about what you could improve.

Remember not to blame yourself.

Every situation is different.

You are trying to improve a lot of things, your ability to:

- Catch yourself and not let your emotions get the best of you,

- Quickly reframe and relax,

- Think of simple statements to buy yourself some time and get help if you can.

Dealing with angry customers is never easy, and it's important to recognize that you did your best in a challenging situation.

Focus on what you learned.

Talk to your supervisor later about why it happened, what can be done differently, and how they prefer you respond.

Maybe even brainstorm other things that could have been done.

The more you think through these situations and practice the techniques, the more natural and automatic they will become.

Keep this book handy as a reference.

Setting Boundaries

Your supervisor might say:

I understand that you're frustrated, but it's not acceptable to speak to our employees that way. Our employees deserve to be treated with respect, just as we try to treat you with respect. Let's start over and talk through this respectfully.

They might even add:

If you need a few minutes to collect your thoughts, please take it. We will be here to work through it with you when you're ready.

Practice this yourself.

You can replace the word employees with "us."

I understand that you're frustrated, but it's not acceptable to speak to us that way. We deserve to be treated with respect, just as we try to treat you with respect. Let's start over and talk through this respectfully. If you need a few minutes to collect your thoughts, please take it. I will be here to work through it with you when you're ready.

How to remember this statement

- Have it on your phone to review if you know a customer is coming in with a problem.
- Have a note card close to take a quick glance if you need to. (Just be discreet)
- Review and practice.
- Chunk it and use an easy acronym: FAIR

Frustration acknowledged

- Chunk 1: "I <u>understand</u> that you're <u>frustrated</u>, but it's <u>not acceptable</u> to <u>speak</u> to our <u>employees</u> that way."

    - Understand

    - Frustrated

    - Not acceptable

    - Speak employees

Acceptable behavior

- Chunk 2: "Our <u>employees</u> <u>deserve</u> to be treated with <u>respect</u>, just as we <u>try</u> to <u>treat you</u> with respect."

    - Employees, Deserve, Respect

    - Try treat you

Invite respect

- o Chunk 3: "Let's <u>start</u> <u>over</u> and <u>talk</u> <u>through</u> this <u>respectfully</u>."
    - Start over
    - Talk through
    - Respectfully

Reflect and restart

- o Chunk 4: "If you need a <u>few</u> <u>minutes</u> to <u>collect</u> your <u>thoughts</u>, please take it. <u>We</u> will be here to <u>work</u> <u>through</u> it with you."
    - Few Minutes
    - Collect thoughts
    - We
    - Work through

Training Card for Setting Boundaries

Training Card Example or Bookmarked Phone Note

I <u>understand</u> that you're <u>frustrated</u>,
but it's <u>not acceptable</u> to <u>speak</u> to our <u>employees</u> that way.
Our <u>employees deserve</u> to be treated with <u>respect</u>,
just as we strive to <u>treat you</u> with respect.
Let's <u>start over</u> and <u>talk through</u> this <u>respectfully</u>
If you need a <u>few minutes</u> to <u>collect</u> your <u>thoughts</u>,
please take it. <u>We</u> will be here to <u>work through</u> it with you."

Frustration Acknowledged	Acceptable behavior
Understand Frustrated Not acceptable Speak employees	Employees, Deserve, Respect Try treat you
Invite respect	Reflect and restart
Start over Talk through Respectfully	Few Minutes Collect thoughts We Work through

Example 3

Someone says,

"Somebody that looks like you would never know what I deal with."

Say, "Oh CRAP, here we go again"

Catch yourself

Reframe it

They're just mean.

Get some Air.

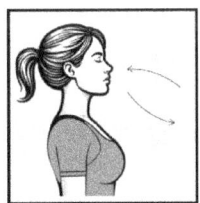 

Take a few breaths. Force yourself to relax.

You could try saying, "We all have things we deal with. If it'll help, tell me what you're feeling."

Here are a few other things you could say in the moment:

"I'm sorry you feel that way. I may not fully understand what you're going through, but I'm willing to listen."

"We all have different challenges. Is there something you're dealing with that you'd like to talk about?"

"I'm sorry if I've given you the impression that I wouldn't understand. Everyone deals with their own difficulties, and I don't want to minimize what you're going through."

Write down a way you might say it

_____

_____

_____

_____

_____

Do your Post event review.

Here is an example of how you could think about the situation:

How did you feel?

      Hurt, angry, defensive?

Remember, don't judge yourself.

Why do you think they acted that way?

      Were they criticized?

      Are they stressed or frustrated?

It doesn't excuse their behavior, but will help you better understand in the future and handle it better internally as well as with what you say.

How did you respond?

Did you catch yourself? Reframe it? Relax?

Remember to practice self compassion.

Navigating these challenging conversations is difficult, and you're doing your best.

Don't dwell on shortcomings, focus on improvement.

Take a softer approach and treat them with care and respect.

It's not about changing the other person's mind.

It's about how you react,

improving,

and

avoiding the negative spiral.

The key to an effective Post event review is to practice.

Keep this book handy.

**You don't need to remember everything,
just where to find it when you need it.**

You've Made it This Far

I have struggled finding the right length for this book to keep it easy to get through, while still including enough detail and repetition to help you remember.

I think that creating follow up books would be best based on the length of the material for those books, but want to make sure you have some of the information here to continue your study, when you're ready.

On the next few pages, I'll summarize some of those key points. There's also a follow up page that provides some excellent sources you can use to get more information.

My goal is to continue covering important topics in the same simple straight forward way this workbook has, so keep an eye out.

If you liked what you read so far,

Let Me Know: **Neal@NealCarboneau.com**

- What was most helpful?

- What could be improved?

- How was the amount of information?
  (Too much at once?)

- Was the conversational style ok?

- What would you like to know more about?

One more thing, please let others know how helpful this book is and encourage them to take a look.

If you bought the book online, please leave a review.

It will help me, and help others decide to take a look.

You can visit my YouTube Page at

www.youtube.com/@NealCarboneau

or my website at www.NealCarboneau.com

A Step Beyond

We talked about starting simple. Just blaming others in the moment when you are re framing.

This will help free up your mind to relax and respond; then, evaluate it later.

But, it's not as easy as blaming someone else. That's just to get you through.

The goal is learning from the situation; understanding yourself and others better.

The other person may be offering constructive criticism, but just doesn't know how to express it.

Here are a few ways you can improve your response and get the best out of each situation.

Improve your

- Self awareness
- Confidence
- Assertiveness and Communication skills

These are all complex topics, but it's important to have a basic understanding. Take a look when you're ready.

Self Awareness

Self awareness is understanding your own thoughts, feelings, and behaviors; as well as, how others see them.

I had a habit of getting a slightly grumpy looking face when I was thinking about something, my thinking face.

My eyebrows would go down and straighten, my nose would wrinkle a little and my jaw would tighten.

These are non verbal signs of irritation.

I never realized it until someone told me they thought I didn't like their idea, when I actually did, but was thinking it through without saying anything.

So people just got the impression I didn't like something when I was just taking a second to think about it.

That's the key to self awareness. Understanding how someone is reacting to you, in the moment.

What is your facial expression right now?

How are you feeling? Tense, Relaxed, Focused?

Try asking yourself those questions at different times.

Understanding nonverbal cues can help you develop greater self awareness and emotional intelligence.

- Body Language, Gestures
- Facial Expressions
- Tone of Voice

Vanessa Van Edwards has excellent information about non verbal communication.

She has YouTube videos and books, as well as other strategies available at:

https://www.scienceofpeople.com/

Her advice can really help you understand your own non verbal cues, how someone may interpret them and how to interpret others' cues. What are they not saying, or how are they feeling in that moment?

Confidence

Confidence is essential for maintaining a positive self image and believing in your abilities.

Cognitive behavioral techniques (CBT), such as challenging negative self talk and practicing positive affirmations, can help boost your self esteem and confidence.

There are a number of YouTube videos on these topics. Look them up when you're ready. Or, ask an Ai LLM.

I mentioned Jim Kwik's book, "Limitless," earlier. He has some great stories about overcoming what we believe is holding us back, as well as strategies to learn faster and retain more. It's worth taking a look. He also has YouTube videos and a website with more information at

https://www.JimKwik.com/

Reflect on your strengths, set achievable goals and understand meaningful change takes time.

Celebrate your successes.

Tap into the confidence already in you.

Effective Communication and Assertiveness

Effective communication and assertiveness are essential skills for navigating personal and professional relationships, especially when facing criticism or conflict.

An example we discussed earlier was setting boundaries. Use that example to help handle tough situations, in the moment, and take back some control.

Being assertive means expressing your thoughts, feelings, and needs in a direct, honest and respectful manner.

By using "I" statements, practicing active listening (listen to understand) and clearly stating your expectations, you can communicate more effectively and maintain healthy relationships.

The following are a few examples of how you can word your comments to respect the other person as well as your thoughts.

These examples have been paraphrased from the sources listed in the Citations Section. Those authors go into much more detail, but here are a few examples to consider.

- "I've noticed that [describe situation]. I'm concerned about [express your worry]. Let's think through some ways we can work through this together?"

- "I understand what you're thinking, but I believe that [state your opinion] because [provide the reason]."

- "I know this is a tough situation. Let's try to find some ways we can work through this that work for both of us."

- "I know you know a lot about this, but I have some thoughts about things I've seen that I think can make this better. Let's talk through them and see if we can find a better solution."

- "I feel uncomfortable when [describe behavior or situation]. It would help if you [state your request] in the future."

  o "I feel uncomfortable when you criticize my work in front of everybody. It would help if you would give me your feedback alone."

- "I value our relationship and want to find a way that works for both of us."

Humor

Humor is another powerful tool in communication but you need to be careful, as it might not be the time for it, or it might be misunderstood.

Making a joke about yourself in the moment might help.

Here's an example

"I'm sorry, I'm learning from my mistakes. I make plenty."

Remember, the key to using humor effectively is to strike a balance between being humble and self aware while still projecting confidence and competence.

Be careful, being too self critical can undermine your credibility and confidence. Use it strategically and in moderation to maintain a healthy balance between humility and self assurance.

If you feel this could be helpful in managing these difficult situations, research it further.

My goal here has been to give you the basic strategies to build from.

Other Ways to Chart Your Course

Some challenges with self improvement include finding simple, inexpensive yet effective sources. Your preference in the style of the author will also impact its usefulness. What I like may be different from what speaks to you. The Citations Section and the referenced file contain a wealth of sources to consider.

YouTube also offers a wide variety of videos on the topics you read about here. Find some that suit you.

As I mentioned, a few of my recent favorites are Jim Kwik and Vanessa Van Edwards.

Paul Scheele is another author that has had a huge impact on my life. His paraliminal recording, "Deep Relaxation," helped me relax and learn effective breathing and relaxation techniques. I have refined these techniques with the guidance in his recording as well as other authors' recommendations. The citations referenced later provide different ways to approach these techniques.

His recordings can be found at

https://www.learningstrategies.com/Paraliminal

We discussed Cognitive Behavioral Therapy (CBT) earlier. It's a powerful therapeutic approach that provides tools for managing negative thinking patterns and emotional responses. While this book introduces some of those approaches, it's important to note that these are simplified adaptations and not a substitute for professional therapy.

If you are interested in exploring CBT further, there are numerous resources available, including YouTube videos and online worksheets. One source I found that has examples you could incorporate in your post event reviews was on the Carepatron website at: https://www.carepatron.com/templates/catastrophizing -worksheet.

However, remember that these resources are for educational purposes only and should not be considered as professional treatment.

To deepen your understanding, you might explore the following CBT related terms through online sources or discussions with Ai language models:

- Catastrophizing: The tendency to assume the worst possible outcome, even when evidence suggests otherwise. Reframe it.

- Automatic Negative Thoughts (ANTs): Spontaneous, often distorted thoughts that arise in response to situations. Recognizing these thoughts is the first step in analyzing their validity. Catch yourself.

- Cognitive Restructuring: A key CBT technique similar to the reframing we've discussed. It involves identifying negative thought patterns and learning to challenge and modify them.

- Behavioral Activation: This concept explores the connection between thoughts, emotions, and behaviors, emphasizing how changing thought patterns can lead to healthier behaviors and improved well being.

While these resources can provide valuable insights and examples to support your personal growth, they are complex, and not replacements for professional help. If you find yourself consistently struggling with negative thought patterns, emotional regulation, or other mental health concerns, it's crucial to seek guidance from a qualified mental health professional, preferably one experienced in CBT techniques.

Remember, seeking professional help is a sign of strength and self care. A trained therapist can provide personalized strategies and support tailored to your specific needs, helping you navigate challenges more effectively and sustainably.

One last thought on finding information tailored to your preferences is to consider using the Ai language models I mentioned earlier to ask specific questions you have.

Here's an example Ai LLM prompt I used to help generate examples of assertive communication based on research and other best practices that I could paraphrase into a statement I felt I would make based on my experience in these situations. You can use this template for this and other topics that are of interest to you.

EXAMPLE Ai LLM PROMPT:

Please provide examples of assertive communication in conversations, drawing from reputable sources in psychology, cognitive science, social psychology, emotional intelligence and conflict resolution. Focus on techniques that are well supported by research and proven effective in real world scenarios.

Include examples that demonstrate:

- Clear expression of thoughts and feelings
- Respect for others' perspectives
- Effective boundary setting
- De-escalation of potential conflicts
- Invitation for collaborative problem solving

Feel free to paraphrase or adapt the language to enhance clarity and applicability. For each example, please cite the source and provide a full MLA citation at the end.

(Prompt Continued on the Next Page)

Some recommended sources to consider, but not limit yourself to:

- Presence: Bringing Your Boldest Self to Your Biggest Challenges by Amy Cuddy
- Getting to Yes by Fisher and Ury
- Emotional Intelligence by Daniel Goleman
- Crucial Conversations by Patterson et al.
- Nonviolent Communication by Marshall Rosenberg
- Negotiating the Nonnegotiable by Daniel Shapiro
- Thanks for the Feedback by Douglas Stone, et al.

Please provide 3-5 diverse examples that showcase different aspects of assertive communication.

(End of the Prompt)

I hope that these suggestions as well as the sources cited at the end of the book provide you with enough ways to find more detailed information on the topics here.

As I mentioned, my hope is to continue refining the information and providing simple straightforward examples like you have experienced here for other related topics, but in the mean time, take a look at the other sources.

The Visionaries that Made Me Who I Am Today

To the visionaries who have profoundly influenced my life and provided the foundation for the strategies for success that I have honed throughout my life: Paul Scheele, Ken Roberts, Vernon Howard, Guy Finley, Jim Collins, Norb Slowikowski, Jim Kwik and Abraham Maslow. Their wisdom, strategies, and commitment to help others on their paths of personal growth have guided me through my journey of self improvement.

Paul Scheele's paraliminal recordings have helped me relax, focus and learn. His book, "PhotoReading," provided strategies to get through large volumes of information in a short time, without sacrificing the necessary detail. I was fortunate to have access to his information early in my life, and it has provided a cornerstone of my personal and professional development.

Ken Roberts was another source for inspiration early in my career. His simple, yet powerful message, to "take the first step" has been a constant source of motivation, reminding me that action is the key to unlocking personal growth and overcoming obstacles.

Recently, I have heard a concept that I think explains this another way: That you don't need motivation, you just need to start.

If you can force yourself to start whatever you have been putting off, your motivation will build just by taking that first step.

Ken also introduced me to Vernon Howard and Guy Finley who also had a profound impact on my life. He said that their knowledge will be worth more than the money I make. I didn't believe it at the time, but have come to realize through them and my continued journey of self improvement that success was internal not external; in who I was, not what I had.

Vernon Howard and Guy Finley taught me how to recognize and observe negative thoughts and emotions which are strategies that have been instrumental in my own growth and success. Learning mindfulness and self awareness has allowed me to live more in the moment, reduce the reflection on negative situations and be able to respond effectively in difficult situations, reducing the emotion and focusing on the situation.

Their strategies have made all the difference in my life.

Jim Collins is a business researcher, educator and writer. His book, "Good to Great," came out early in my career and helped me understand the strategies for business success. It also laid out what makes a good leader which guided my business success and provided a foundation for the strategies I have honed throughout my life.

His discussion of the "Flywheel Effect" tied in well with Ken Roberts' comment to "take the first step," and other authors' refinement of the principles to get motivated and keep going.

Once you start pushing that flywheel, it will gain speed and take less effort to continue.

Jim also discusses the "doom loop" in business which I thought was an appropriate term for those negative thoughts replaying in our minds, the negative spiral.

Jim Collins and Norb Slowikowski together have had a significant impact on my life. Their educational backgrounds, research and application of psychology in business have shaped my understanding and approach to leadership and management.

Norb's book "Hard-Hat Productivity: The 9 Critical Factors for Maximizing Profits" was a pivotal work that drew on his background in psychology and practical experience in industry to brilliantly articulate many of the lessons I had learned firsthand.

His practical writing style and focus on human centered management resonated deeply with me.

Hearing Norb speak about his work with McDonald's and how his productivity studies could be incorporated in effective leadership and management strategies further cemented the understanding I had with the underlying principles.

He explains how efficiency, effectiveness, employee satisfaction and customer service can all work together to form a positive organizational culture.

These insights helped me better understand and articulate my own ideas about human centered leadership and management. His work was instrumental in bridging my experience in construction and engineering with the psychological aspects of success. Norb's book not only influenced my thinking, but also served as an inspiring model when I set out to write my own book, showing me how complex ideas could be communicated in a simple and practical way. I want to express my sincere thanks to Norb for his wisdom and its impact on my life.

Abraham Maslow's groundbreaking work on human motivation and the hierarchy of needs tied in well with these concepts and further supported my understanding of leadership and motivation.

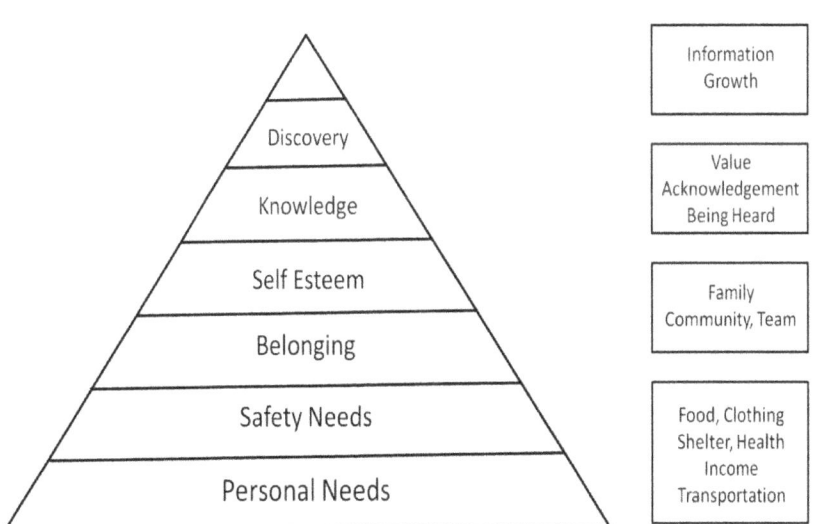

Finally, I recently found Jim Kwik's book, "Limitless." It was equally as profound in its guidance as the other authors. Jim's life story and strategies have helped me refine my strategies for success and be more productive, even amongst the hardships I currently face.

He provides simple strategies to help others escape digital distraction, get their life back and unlock their full potential.

Jim also pulls together some of the best strategies I have learned over a lifetime in one place, and makes them simple to learn and understand.

To all of these authors, I extend my heartfelt appreciation for the impact you have made on my life and the lives of countless others. Your teachings have not only transformed my personal and professional journey but have also served as the foundation for the creation of this book.

It is my sincere hope that the strategies, techniques, and insights compiled within these pages will help readers navigate the challenges of criticism, build emotional resilience, and unlock their true potential. By drawing from a wide range of disciplines and personal experiences, this book aims to provide a comprehensive and practical guide to personal growth and self improvement.

Just as these authors' wisdom has illuminated my path, I hope that the content of this book has the power to transform lives and inspire readers to embrace their own journey of self discovery. I have learned that with the right tools, mindset, and support, we all have the capacity to overcome adversity, cultivate inner peace, and succeed in ways we never thought possible.

The Technology Changing the World

In the creation of this book, I would like to acknowledge the invaluable role played by artificial intelligence (Ai) language models: Anthropic's Claude.ai, Open Ai's Chat GPT, Microsoft's Copilot and Google's Gemini. These cutting edge tools have been instrumental in the research, refinement, analysis and the artwork that brings this resource to life. By leveraging the power of Ai, I have been able to develop a comprehensive, yet easy to understand, book that empowers readers to navigate the complexities of dealing with criticism and cultivating emotional resilience.

Ai's ability to process vast amounts of information, identify key insights, tailor them to my perspective and experience and help me present them in a clear and engaging manner has been a game changer in the development of this book. Thanks to these advanced language models, the content is organized and presented in a way that ensures readers can easily understand and apply the proven, evidence based strategies and techniques presented, regardless of their previous experience with the topic.

The Ai LLMs have also helped me maintain a conversational yet professional tone throughout the book. By striking this balance, the material becomes easy to read and apply for a wide range of readers, from those just beginning their self improvement journey to seasoned professionals seeking to enhance their skills and knowledge.

I am truly astounded by the capabilities of Ai. As I continue to explore this technology, I envision creating a suite of supplemental content, such as audio, video, and online training materials, to provide a variety of ways learners can access the information.

I also plan to release future volumes that will delve into self awareness and communication. These upcoming books will build upon the foundation laid here, providing the next steps in readers' journey of personal growth and success.

My ultimate goal is to complete a transformational leadership program that builds on my experience in leadership and management as well as the psychological principles that drive success. This program would emphasize the importance of leaders understanding those they lead and be founded on mastering self awareness and emotional intelligence.

The Power of Personal Growth

As I reflect on my journey of self improvement, the creation of my training programs and this book, I am filled with a deep sense of gratitude for the experiences, both challenging and rewarding, that have shaped my path. My story is one of resilience, determination and a steadfast belief in the power of personal growth, a story that I hope will inspire and empower you, to embrace your own journey of self discovery.

Early in my career, I discovered the value of self improvement. The wisdom and guidance of visionaries like Paul Scheele, Ken Roberts, Vernon Howard, Guy Finley, Jim Collins, Abraham Maslow and Jim Kwik, illuminated my path and provided me with the tools and mindset necessary to overcome obstacles and achieve success. Their teachings, which emphasized the importance of self awareness, resilience and continuous learning, became the foundation upon which I built my personal and professional life.

Inspired by the impact these individuals had on my own growth, I set out to share their wisdom with others by building a small training business. The experience of working closely with participants and witnessing their transformative journeys was incredibly fulfilling.

I poured my heart and soul into creating practical, concise, yet comprehensive, training content that resonated with my audience. The feedback I received was nothing short of amazing.

Participants would often share heartfelt comments like, "No one in business has ever cared about me as much as you," or "I never expected this kind of impact on my operations." Some would express their initial doubts and subsequent breakthroughs, saying, "I never thought I could do this. Your step by step guidance and motivation made all the difference." Others would praise the relevance and practicality of the material, noting, "Your understanding of what we do is spot on. Your tips and guidance will be invaluable." These words of appreciation fueled my passion for helping others and reaffirmed my belief in the power of self improvement.

However, life had unexpected challenges in store for me. When the COVID-19 pandemic struck, it brought my thriving training business to an end. I contracted COVID in the early days and have been living with long COVID ever since. The financial and physical toll was devastating, as I found myself grappling with the loss of my livelihood, financial stability and the catastrophic effects of long COVID.

In the face of these overwhelming obstacles, I was forced to confront my own resilience and rely on the strategies I have been learning over a lifetime to survive. I found the strength to persevere and the clarity to chart a new course forward. Step by step, I began to rebuild, working part time to survive and channeling what energy I had left into researching, analyzing, refining and writing this book.

The process of creating this book was not only therapeutic but also transformative. By leveraging the power and speed of Ai language models, I was able to tap into a vast wealth of knowledge in psychology, cognitive science, and behavioral science and relate it back to my experience and goals of creating simple, practical guidance to develop this book.

This collaboration allowed me to develop comprehensive and evidence based guidance that I believe will make a meaningful difference in the lives of others.

Throughout the writing process, I found myself reflecting on my own experiences and the lessons I had learned along the way.

The act of researching and writing with the help of the Ai reinforced my belief that simple yet comprehensive and practical strategies can be developed for complex situations.

The power of self awareness, resilience and continuous improvement has served me well and provided a foundation for this book and my other programs.

This process also deepened my empathy for others who are struggling in life. I have always been keenly aware of others' struggles as I travelled the country consulting and providing training. My recent part time job amplified that understanding and was the spark to help others struggling with criticism, setbacks or self doubt.

My personal journey, with its triumphs and trials, has fueled my desire to make self improvement resources practical, easy to understand and widely available. I firmly believe that everyone deserves the opportunity to tap into their full potential and lead a life of purpose and fulfillment.

By sharing my story and the strategies that have helped me overcome adversity, I hope to inspire and empower readers to embark on their own path of personal growth.

As you make your way on your path of
self improvement, know that you are not alone.

Like you, I have faced challenges that seemed insurmountable at times. But through the power of self improvement and the support of those who have guided me along the way, I was able to use that inner strength and resilience to forge a path to success through hardship.

It is my sincerest hope that this book will serve as a beacon of light and a source of guidance as you navigate your own journey of self discovery. May the strategies, techniques and insights within these pages empower you to embrace your own resilience, to face criticism with grace and understanding and to continuously grow and evolve as an individual.

Remember, your story is still unfolding, and every challenge you face is an opportunity to learn, grow and transform. Embrace the journey, trust in your own strength and know that you have the power within you to overcome any obstacle and achieve your dreams.

The Strength to Move Forward

As you've read through my personal story and the lessons I've learned along the way, you may have found yourself relating to some of the challenges and struggles I've faced. Whether you're dealing with criticism, navigating change or overcoming setbacks, know that you're not alone in your journey. Just as I've had to confront obstacles like building and losing a business or struggling with the ongoing effects of long COVID, you too may be facing difficulties that seem overwhelming at times.

But here's the truth, you have within you the strength, resilience and potential to overcome any challenge that comes your way. The strategies and techniques outlined in this book, which have been crucial in my own journey of self improvement, can be applied to your own life to help you build the emotional intelligence and resilience needed to thrive in the face of adversity.

Take, for example, the simple statement, "oh CRAP, here we go again," a simple yet powerful tool for managing your response to criticism or self doubt. By learning to Catch yourself, Reframe your thoughts, get some Air, and conduct a Post event review, you can transform the way you handle critical feedback and use it as an opportunity for growth and development.

Similarly, the self awareness exercises and mindfulness techniques presented in this book can help you cultivate a deeper understanding of your own thoughts, emotions and behaviors, empowering you to make positive changes and build stronger relationships.

But, the journey of self improvement doesn't end with the last page of this book. In fact, it's just the beginning. The key to lasting personal growth lies in continuous learning, self reflection and the consistent application of the principles and strategies you've learned. By making a commitment to yourself and your own development, you can continue to build upon the foundation laid in this book and create a life of purpose, fulfillment and success.

Remember, every challenge you face is an opportunity to learn, grow and become the best version of yourself. With perseverance, self compassion and a commitment to your own development, there is no limit to what you can achieve.

As Ken Roberts said, "take the first step."

I really hope this book serves as the spark for change in your life. I believe in you and your ability to transform your life for the better.

The path forward is yours to create, and I am honored to be a part of that journey.

Here's to building a brighter future, one characterized by self awareness, emotional intelligence and the courage to face any challenge that comes your way. The first step starts now, and I'm excited about where it will take you.

A Little About Me

I wanted to share some of my background to help you understand my experience as well as the path that has lead me here.

I grew up in Rolling Prairie, Indiana and currently live near Three Oaks, Michigan. I earned a degree in Civil Engineering from Purdue University and later became licensed as a professional engineer.

I spent seventeen years in the road and bridge construction industry and fifteen, to date, providing training and technical assistance in leadership, operations and management.

Throughout that time, I continued to study self improvement techniques and the psychological principles that support those techniques.

I have always had a passion for helping others; whether it be helping others in the construction industry better understand the work or training participants in my classes on simple, easy to apply strategies.

Throughout my years learning, working and training, I honed simple yet effective strategies for success, which I incorporated in my training programs as well as this book to help others learn and apply these strategies faster and easier than I did.

I have always tried to support those strategies with evidence based principles to help others better understand why they are so effective.

But, understanding that information has no value unless it's being used, I wanted to start offering some of these strategies in a widely available format, which is why I started with this book and will follow up with videos and other online resources.

Having made it this far, you also probably realize that I have tried to maintain a simple, down to earth, conversational style.

I believe it's easier to read, understand, and connect with.

I hope that what it has taken me a lifetime to understand and simplify, will take root quickly in you and allow you to succeed faster and more abundantly that me.

Citations

A full alphabetical list of the sources you may want to consider for further study is available in my Google Drive folder at the following address:

https://bit.ly/3NaTFzR

Foundational Sources:

Finley (2006); Finley (2007); Finley (2008); Finley (2010); Howard (1965); Howard (1967); Howard (1968); Kwik (2020); Marcinko (1996); Maslow (1954); Roberts (1995); Scheele (1990's); Scheele (1995); Howard (2011)

Breathing and Relaxation Techniques:

Benson & Klipper (1975); Brown & Gerbarg (2005); Busch et al. (2012); Chugh-Gupta et al. (2013); Divine & Divine (2016); Jerath et al. (2006); Kabat-Zinn (1990); Ma et al. (2017); Russo et al. (2017); Schuman (2020); Zaccaro et al. (2018); Zope & Zope (2013)

Cognitive Behavioral Approaches:

Beck (1976); Beck et al. (1979); Burns (1980); Ellis & Harper (1961); Hendriksen (2021); Kabat-Zinn (1990); Linehan (1993); Musek (2022); Neff (2011); Seligman (1991)

Citations Continued

Coping with Criticism and Resilience:

Carnegie (1936); Chu (2019); Dweck (2006); Greitens (2015); Holt (2020); Kjærvik & Bushman (2023); Lambertsen (2023); Meier (2024); Nolen-Hoeksema (2000); Nolen-Hoeksema et al. (2008); Troy et al. (2010)

Emotional Detachment

Cuddy (2015); Fisher & Ury (1981); Goleman (1995); Patterson et al., (2012); Rosenberg (2015); Shapiro (2017); Stone & Heen (2015)

Emotional Intelligence and Self Awareness:

Cannon (1915); Damasio (1994); Ekman & Friesen (1975); Goleman (1995); Gross (2002); Lazarus & Folkman (1984); LeDoux (1996); Ochsner & Gross (2005); Sajnani & Johnson (2000); Schachter & Singer (1962); Selye (1956)

Mindfulness and Present Moment Awareness:

"How to Develop Present Moment Awareness" (2022); Kabat-Zinn (1990); Linehan (1993); Manotas (2016); Seppälä et al. (2020); "The Art of Now" (2008)

Citations Continued

Post Event Review and Growth Mindset:

Cacioppo & Patrick (2008); Cloud & Townsend (2017); Dweck (2006); Eurich (2017); Germer (2009); Leahy (2015); Malejko et al. (2017); Stone & Heen (2015); Trapnell & Campbell (1999); Tugend (2012); Watkins (2008)

Stress, Trauma and Emotional Healing:

Almeida et al. (2018); Bockarova (2020); Cohen & Lansing (2022); Cozolino (2014); Davis (2020); Germer (2009); "Healing the Invisible Wounds" (2023); Herman (1997); Levine (1997); McQueeney (2017); Porges (2011); Robinson et al. (2024); Sapolsky (1994); Schwartz et al. (2020); Taylor et al. (2000); "Types of Emotional Wounds" (2023); Van der Kolk (2015); Wright et al. (2019)

Assertive Communication

Cuddy (2015); Fisher & Ury (1981); Goleman (1995); Patterson et al. (2012); Rosenberg (2015); Shapiro (2017); Stone & Heen (2015)

One last Reminder,

if you liked what you read so far,

Let Me Know: **Neal@NealCarboneau.com**

- What was most helpful?

- What could be improved?

- How was the amount of information?
  (Too much at once?)

- Was the conversational style easy to read?

- What would you like to know more about?

In closing, I would sincerely appreciate it if you would let others know how helpful this book is and encourage them to take a look.

If you bought the book online, please leave a review.

It will help me, and help others decide to take a look.

You can visit my YouTube Page at www.youtube.com/@NealCarboneau or my website at www.NealCarboneau.com

www.ingramcontent.com/pod-product-compliance
Lightning Source LLC
Chambersburg PA
CBHW051544120626
46551CB00013B/1356